LONDON
HEATHROW

LONDON
HEATHROW
THE WORLD'S BUSIEST INTERNATIONAL AIRPORT

FREDDY BULLOCK

Airlife
England

First published in the UK in 1999
by Airlife Publishing Ltd

British Library Cataloguing-in-Publication Data
A catalogue record for this book
is available from the British Library

ISBN 1 84037 099 8

Typeset by Rowland Phototypesetting Ltd,
Bury St Edmunds, Suffolk.
Printed in Hong Kong.

Airlife Publishing Ltd
101 Longden Road, Shrewsbury, SY3 9EB, England
E-mail: airlife@airlifebooks.com
Website: www.airlifebooks.com

London Heathrow Airport

Heathrow's place in history can be traced back to a Celtic-Roman temple which was excavated in 1944, but pottery discovered here dates back to 300BC. Once a forest, the land was cleared in the 13th Century by King Henry III to create a heath. The hamlet which grew here has been called Heathrowe, Headrowe and its present name.

In the 17th Century the area was used by stagecoaches travelling to and from London. This in turn attracted highwaymen, the most notorious gang being led by a Molly Cutpurse. The legendary Dick Turpin is also reputed to have worked in the area. Many were caught and hanged on Tyburn Tree and their remains were placed on a gibbet at Hounslow Heath.

Moving forward to this century it was in 1927 that the Fairey Aviation Company purchased 150 acres of land near Heathrow village to build and test their aircraft. The area became known as the 'Great West Aerodrome'.

It was during World War II however, that the Government began a search for a site suitable for a military aerodrome capable of expansion to cover the need for a supply base for Far East operations. Pressure was also mounting for a new civil airport to replace Croydon, which was unsuitable for further expansion. The Government decided that Heathrow was perfect for their plans and in May 1944 a compulsory purchase order was issued to the local council for the purchase of 2,800 acres of land. Work started in June of that year on the construction of the runways.

On 1 January 1946, and still a vast building site, Heathrow was transferred from military to civilian use. That same day a British South American Airways converted Lancaster bomber left on a proving flight to Buenos Aires with six crew and ten passengers. After fuelling stops in Lisbon, Bathurst in West Africa and Natal in Brazil, its destination was reached 35 hours later. Heathrow was officially opened on 31 May that same year, when the first aircraft to land was a BOAC Lancastrian on a flight from Australia, followed by a Pan American Lockheed Constellation, which had flown the Atlantic route. At this time Heathrow consisted of a tented village with limited facilities by today's standards, but by the end of the year 60,000 passengers and 2,400 tons of freight had been carried.

On 2 May 1952 the Jet age arrived with a flight to Johannesburg flown by a BOAC Comet 1. Expansion at Heathrow has continued ever since. April 1955 saw the opening of the 'Europa Building' now (Terminal 2), the 'Queen's Building' and a new Air Traffic Control tower. The 'Oceanic Building', now (Terminal 3) followed in November 1961. Terminal 1 was opened in 1968 to cater for all short-haul flights.

The management of the airport was transferred from the Ministry of Civil

Aviation to a newly created British Airports Authority in April 1966, which was then privatised in 1987. From that time BAA Plc, as it is now known, has expanded rapidly both at home and overseas.

By the late 70s it had become clear that further major development at Heathrow would need to be focused outside the Central Terminal Area, which resulted in Terminal 4 being built on the south-east side of the airfield. Terminal 4 opened in 1986 and is used primarily by British Airways and its code-share partner airlines for intercontinental services. Plans are presently being considered for a fifth terminal at the western end of the airport to cater for the continuing demand for air travel now and into the 21st Century. Heathrow can successfully claim to be the world's busiest international airport.

There are three runways at Heathrow comprising the Northern (09L/27R), which is 3,658 metres long, the Southern (09R/27L) at 3,902 metres in length and the rarely used Crosswind (05/23) at 1,966 metres.

In the 12 months to October 1998, almost 60 million passengers were handled at Heathrow and cargo tonnage amounted to 1,216,129 metric tonnes. Aircraft movements for the same period were 439,250.

BAA Plc have a continuing programme of investment at Heathrow with £1 million per day being spent on facilities and customer service developments. This has included the opening of the *Heathrow Express* fast rail link to London's Paddington Station in June 1998. *Heathrow Express* is proving to be a great success, with its journey time of just 15 minutes, every 15 minutes to Central London. At the present time 34% of passengers using Heathrow arrive by public transport, more than any other airport in the world.

Heathrow is a vast business enterprise employing 57,000 people on the airport and another 23,000 in the surrounding area. The airport generates over £3 billion in wages per year.

I hope readers will enjoy this book, which aims to show the majority of airlines using this exciting airport. My sincere thanks go to Sir John Egan, Chief Executive Officer of BAA Plc, for his assistance. Thanks also go to my wife, Chris, who has given me much support, David Apps of British Airways and I am indebted to Darryl Bartlette, BAA Heathrow Public Affairs, for the many efforts he has made on my behalf.

Freddy Bullock
Huddersfield, England

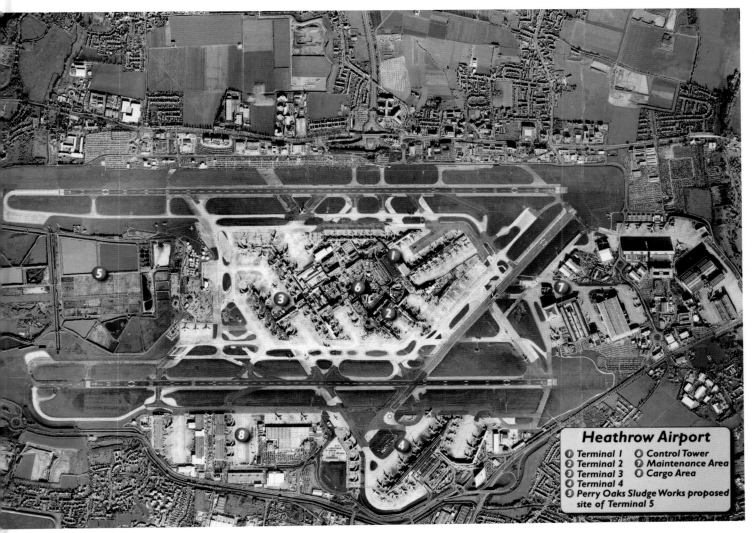

Heathrow Airport

1. Terminal 1
2. Terminal 2
3. Terminal 3
4. Terminal 4
5. Perry Oaks Sludge Works proposed site of Terminal 5
6. Control Tower
7. Maintenance Area
8. Cargo Area

An aerial view of London Heathrow, which clearly shows the layout of the airport. The Northern runway 09L/27R is at the top of the photograph with the Southern runway 09R/27L in the lower part. The rarely used Crosswind runway 05/23 is also seen. (BAA)

With the British Airways Concorde mock-up on the left of the picture, we see the road tunnel entrance to Terminals 1, 2 and 3, situated at the centre of the airport.

Heathrow can be reached by car, taxi, underground railway and bus. This Heathrow Airbus shuttle operated by London Transport waits outside Terminal 2 for passengers.

A view of Terminal 2 which caters for all European flights operated by non-British airlines. The Queen's Building can be seen to the left.

The British Airports Authority recently opened the Heathrow Visitor's Centre, depicting the history of the airport and all its operations. It has proved immensely popular with the general public and is well worth a visit. This building is situated on the A4 Bath Road just outside the airfield. Free buses from the airport's bus station are available. (BAA)

A view of the British Midland check-in
counters situated within Terminal 1.

Garfunkel's bar situated within Terminal 2.

The only remaining old-style arrivals board tells its own story, and is situated at Terminal 3.

flight	from	last stop	due	expected	landed	information
BG007	DHAKA	ROME	12:05		12:25	BAGGAGE IN HALL
SK1513	OSLO		12:05		12:20	BAGGAGE IN HALL
UA934	HONOLULU	LOS ANGELES	12:25		12:55	BAGGAGE IN HALL
RG762	RIO DE JANEIRO	SAO PAULO	12:30			LANDED 1315
MS777	CAIRO		12:35			LANDED 1252
SK531	STOCKHOLM		12:45		12:35	BAGGAGE IN HALL
KU101	KUWAIT		13:00		12:50	BAGGAGE IN HALL
AA136	LOS ANGELES		13:05		12:15	BAGGAGE IN HALL
NH201	TOKYO		14:50			EXPECTED 1410
CA937	BEIJING		15:00			EXPECTED 1425
JL421	OSAKA		15:20			EXPECTED 1445
VS024	LOS ANGELES		15:30			EXPECTED 1433

Passengers ending their journey in this terminal normally leave the Customs Hall approximately 40 minutes after the time of landing

The departure hall in Terminal 2.

With the abolition of duty-free shopping within the European Union, BAA will continue to offer passengers goods at tax-free and duty-free prices.

Deep underground is the jewel of BAA's continued improvement to the facilities at the airport. Opened in 1998, the *Heathrow Express* is an electric train service which travels to and from Paddington Station in the capital offering a journey time of 15 minutes.

British Midland are the ground-handling
agents of the Spanish airline Aviaco.
Baggage handlers are in the process of
loading the company's McDonnell-Douglas
MD-88 EC-FOG.

Situated to the west of Terminal 3 is the Airport Operations building, the control centre for all maintenance relating to runways and apron areas. An example of the vehicles used is this Range Rover.

This view of Heathrow's Air Traffic Control Tower was taken from the spectators' terrace looking north. This facility, opened in 1955, is responsible for all flight operations.

Opposite: The Civil Aviation Authority are responsible for all Air Traffic Control throughout the British Isles. This picture shows part of the interior of their control tower at London Heathrow, from where all movements relating to approach and ground movements are monitored. (CAA)

Fire tender number 2 of the British Airport
Authorities Airport Fire Service stands
outside the control room which operates
the 'Green Goddess' (see page 22)
simulator.

With an impressive array of fire-fighting equipment, Heathrow is able to deal with any emergency that may arise. The three tenders shown are lined up at their sub-station within Terminal 2.

Nicknamed the 'Green Goddess', this cross between a Boeing 747 and DC-10 is BAA's new £4 million state-of-the-art fire-fighting simulator. Computer controlled and using propane gas, a fire can be created anywhere inside and out of the module, as this engine fire illustrates.

Opposite: These two scenes show the airport fire service at work on a real practice drill using the new simulator. (BAA)

Baggage containers are being loaded onto
this Iberia Airbus A300, EC-DLG, prior to
the start of Flight IB3163 to Madrid.

An interesting museum piece hidden away in a quiet corner of the airport is this Trident 3, painted in the present-day British Airways scheme, still bearing its original registration G-AWZK. Although its wings have been clipped it is well cared for by the preservation team of British Airways employees.

British Airways Boeing 737-436, G-DOCB,
is inches from touchdown on runway 27L.
This aircraft wears the Danish design
entitled 'Wings'.

Poland's contribution to the British Airways world tail markings scheme is entitled 'Koguty Lowickie' and displayed on the company's Boeing 737-436, G-DOCF, seen here in landing mode.

Above: 'Grand Union', based on an English design, is seen on the tail of British Airways Boeing 757-236 G-BMRJ, on finals for runway 09L.

Opposite above: G-MEDA is one of three Airbus A320-231s which started services with British Mediterranean Airways operating to and from Lebanon. Now flying under the British Airways banner, this aircraft with its 'Whale Rider' tail scheme originating from Canada is seen approaching 27R on Flight BA6702 from Beirut.

Opposite below: This British Airways Boeing 757-236, G-BIKA, is making its way to runway 27R for the start of another shuttle flight to Manchester. The tail scheme is another English design entitled 'Blue Poole'.

The Swedish 'Blomsterang' ('Flower Fields') tail-scheme is illustrated on this British Airways Boeing 757-236, G-BMRI, which is being pushed back from the gate at Terminal 1.

Opposite: Another example of the Swedish design 'Blomsterang' is featured on the tail of this British Airways Boeing 747-236B, G-BDXG.

Opposite above: Only a few weeks out of the paint shop, British Airways Boeing 767-336ER, G-BNWJ, looks superb with its Russian-inspired tail artwork entitled 'Golden Khokhloma'. It is taxying towards runway 27R for take-off.

Opposite below: British Airways Boeing 767-336ER G-BZHC.

'Waves and Cranes' is the Japanese contribution to the tail of this British Airways Boeing 767-336ER, G-BZHC. With Terminal 3 in the background, the aircraft is taxying for take-off.

'Tails.' A British Airways line-up shows the 'Benyhone Tartan' on the Boeing 777 in the foreground, then 'Delftblue Daybreak,' a Dutch design, on a Boeing 747, followed by the standard scheme on another Boeing 747.

Opposite above: British Airways Boeing 777-236, G-VIIA, is seen parked at the engine run-up bay within the company's own engineering facility. The 'Waves of the City' emblem is an American design.

Opposite below: It would appear that a blue nose-cone was not available when this Boeing 777-236, G-ZZZB, was in maintenance, hence the white substitute. It is seen taxying from Terminal 4.

Above : British Airways Boeing 747-436, G-BNLS, sporting the Aboriginal artwork entitled 'Wanula Dreaming' floats gracefully through the air on its final approach to runway 09L.

Opposite: G-BNLS is seen again. A company 'Triple Seven' is in the backgound.

This imposing British Airways Boeing 747-236, G-BDXC, made the author feel very small by comparison as it passed.

Opposite above: An example of the Hong Kong-inspired Chinese calligraphy motif entitled 'Rendezvous' is seen on British Airways Boeing 747-436, G-CIVV, as it slowly taxies to runway 09R for take-off.

Opposite below: Looking quite superb with its 'Chelsea Rose' tail scheme, this British Airways Boeing 747-236B is on the taxiway from Terminal 4 leading to the threshold of runway 09R.

Opposite and above: Entitled 'Colum', this tail design originating in Eire is worn by British Airways Boeing 747-436, G-CIVP. It is at the gate in Terminal 4 loading with passengers and baggage in preparation for its flight.

British Airways Concorde, G-BOAD, is undergoing routine maintenance in the company's hangar at Heathrow.

Opposite above: British Airways flagship service to New York JFK is flown twice-daily by Concorde, offering its passengers a flight that takes less than four hours. With its call sign 'Speedbird Concorde 002', G-BOAA sporting the new 'Union Flag' on its tail, is seen about to land on 27L.

Opposite below: On a poor November day beneath a leaden sky, British Airways Concorde, G-BOAA, moves away from its gate in Terminal 1 at the start of a special charter flight.

British Midland's Boeing 737-59D G-BVZF has completed its push-back from gate 'Bravo 2' at Terminal 1 and will now be requesting permission to proceed with Flight BD414, the 11.35 departure to Leeds/Bradford Airport.

A British Midland Boeing 737-59D.

46

BMA – British Midland Airways – are one of the major operators using Heathrow with an ever-expanding route network. Boeing 737-37Q G-ODSK has taxied round the northern side from Terminal 1 and is seen at block 59 en route for take-off.

Opposite: Introduced into service with the airline in 1998, the Airbus A321 provides additional capacity for British Midland on its busier routes. G-MIDF is seen on finals for runway 09L.

The crisp emerald-and-white scheme of
Aer Lingus looks resplendent on this front-
end view of their Boeing 737-448, EI-BXC.

BAC 1-11s are now very rare visitors to Heathrow, so G-AVMK in Jersey European colours made a splendid sight at Terminal 2 during the autumn of 1998. This aircraft, originally operated by British Airways, would have been a regular visitor to Heathrow in the '70s.

This Boeing 737-33A of Virgin Express,
registered OO-LTU, lifts off the runway and
begins its flight to Brussels.

Familiar sights at the airport are the Airbus A340s used by Virgin Atlantic on international services. G-VFAR is being towed to a gate at Terminal 3 in preparation for its next flight.

Ladybird is the name adorning this Virgin Atlantic Boeing 747-41R, registered G-VAST. It is taxying to the gate at Terminal 3 after landing.

Looking superb in the afternoon sun, Virgin Atlantic's Boeing 747-41R G-VAST awaits further instructions from the tower before proceeding to its gate at Terminal 3.

Air Canada's Boeing 747-233B SCD, C-GAGB, is pushed back from the gate at the start of Flight AC857 to Toronto.

Canadian Boeing 767-375ER C-GSCA is
temporarily parked away from the
terminals until its next flight.

From time to time special charters fly into Heathrow and this was the case with Air Transit's Lockheed TriStar 500. After spending several days parked in the cargo area C-GTSP is being loaded with provisions in readiness for its return flight to Canada.

Opposite: Late arriving at Heathrow, due to bad weather in the United States, American Airlines Airbus A300 is just about to touch down on runway 27L.

This Boeing 767-322ER, N653UA, is United Airlines contribution to the 'Star Alliance' code-sharing scheme (see page 119) and shows the six airline partners involved. Next to go from runway 09R, final instuctions are awaited from the control tower.

Another major user of the Boeing 'Triple Seven', the American airline United has many flights per day from Heathrow across 'The Pond' (Atlantic Ocean). Flight UA921 is a non-stop service to Washington Dulles, which today will be flown by N770UA, shown at the gate to Terminal 3.

British West Indies Airlines TriStar 500s have been regular visitors to Heathrow for many years. 9Y-TGN gathers speed down runway 09R for take-off to Barbados, with Flight BW901.

Opposite: Probably the most colourful aircraft to regularly visit Heathrow is this Airbus A310-324, N837AB, of Air Jamaica. Operating Flight JM002 to Kingston, N837AB is taxying towards runway 27R.

The Brazilian airline Varig recently introduced a new modern image for their aircraft. McDonnell-Douglas MD-11 PP-VPL, sporting the new scheme, taxies out of Terminal 3 at the start of its return flight to Rio de Janeiro.

With Ghana Airways DC-10 not available for Flight GH731 to Accra, the company leased this Bellview Airbus A300B4-622R, 5N-BVU, from the Nigerian charter company to operate the service. Seen at Terminal 3, the aircraft is being loaded with catering provisions for the flight.

This is Terminal 4 where the gateway has just been retracted from an Airbus A340. Flight UL506 of Air Lanka is requesting permission from the tower for 'push' at the start of the flight to Colombo.

Opposite above: Air-India Flight 184 to Dehli prepares for take-off to the east with a Boeing 747-437. This aircraft is a combi-variant, carrying seven pallets of freight in the rear passenger section.

Opposite below: A front-end view of Pakistan International's Boeing 747-217B, AP-BCL.

Syrianair's Boeing 747SP-94, YK-AHA, turns onto the threshold of runway 09R in preparation for its flight to Damascus. This photograph was taken in August 1976 and the aircraft continues to visit Heathrow to this day.

Opposite above: After push-back from the gate at Terminal 3 Kuwait Airways' Boeing 777-269, 9K-AOB, waits to taxi at the start of Flight KU102, scheduled to depart at 11.30 for Kuwait City.

Opposite below: On another day Kuwait Airways Airbus A340-313, 9K-ANA, was being used on Flight KU102

The Saudi Government operate a large fleet of aircraft, which are used for VIP flights to many parts of the world. Their Gulfstream 3, HZ-HFU, is such an example and is parked awaiting its next flight.

Seen here on finals to land at Heathrow is
El Al's Boeing 747-258B, 4X-AXC, operating
Flight LY0315 from Tel Aviv.

Iran Air's Boeing 747SP-86, EP-IAC, has been visiting Heathrow for 20 years and still looks superb. Just turning onto runway 09R in the late afternoon, Flight IR710 will fly non-stop to the Iranian capital, Tehran, arriving at 02.10 local time.

Opposite above: 'Ready to go.' Operating Flight number BI098, Royal Brunei's Boeing 767-33AER, V8-RBJ, eases its brakes and starts to roll down runway 09R at the beginning of its flight to Bandar Seri Begawan.

Opposite below: V8-RBJ was also photographed sitting at the gate at Terminal 3.

This Boeing 747SP-27, owned by the Oman Government, represents the ultimate in luxury with its first-class facilities, including addirional satellite communications, which are housed in the bulge on the top of the fuselage.

Opposite above: To increase capacity Ghana Airways leased this McDonnell-Douglas DC-10-30, 9G-PHN, from the Belgium airline Skyjet. It is seen taxying for take-off with Flight GH731 to the country's capital, Accra.

Opposite below: The Boeing 777 is becoming increasingly popular with the world's airlines. This Boeing 777-21H, A6-EMG, has just arrived at Heathrow on Flight EK001, flying non-stop from Dubai. It is now making its way to the stand in Terminal 3.

Regularly flying from the city of Tangiers on Tuesdays and Saturdays, Flight AT802 is about to land at Heathrow, flown by Royal Air Maroc's Boeing 737-4B6, CN-RNA.

Opposite above: State of Qatar's Airbus A340-211, A7-AHK, displays its colours on final approach for landing.

Opposite below: Wearing the new desert sand livery, this Boeing 777-268, HZ-AKA, of Saudi Arabian Airlines taxies towards runway 27R for take-off on Flight SV0112 to Jeddah.

Egyptair's Boeing 777-236, SU-GBP, in the airline's new colour scheme, is moments away from touchdown on runway 27R, operating Flight MS777 which flies daily non-stop from Cairo.

Opposite above: Gulf Air's Airbus A340-312, A40-LE, arrives from Abu Dhabi.

Opposite below: Despite the dull weather it was a delight to see and photograph this

Nigerian Government Boeing 727-2N6, 5N-FGN, after its arrival from Lagos carrying the country's President. This type is very rarely seen at Heathrow.

After flying overnight from Nairobi and disembarking its passengers in Terminal 4, Kenya Airways Airbus A310-304, 5Y-BEN, is towed to the cargo area where freight containers are loaded and unloaded.

Opposite above: Arriving from Johannesburg in the early morning, Boeing 747-312 ZS-SAC has been towed from the terminal to spend the day in a quieter area of Heathrow prior to its departure later in the day.

Opposite below: This front-end picture of South African's Boeing 747-444, ZS-SAX, illustrates the new clean-cut image of the airline.

Opposite above: Beautifully lit in the late afternoon sunshine, Air Mauritius Airbus A340-313X 3B-NBD turns onto the threshold of runway 09R to operate Flight MK053, a service flying non-stop to Mauritius.

Opposite below: Recently arrived from Beirut, Middle East Airlines' (MEA) Airbus A310-222, 3B-STJ, taxies to its gate within Terminal 3.

Flying a twice-daily service to Singapore, Singapore Airlines Boeing 747-412, 9V-SME, is taxying to its take-off position ready for Flight SQ319, the midday departure.

Opposite above: McDonnell-Douglas MD-11F of MAS Kargo, the freight arm of Malaysia Airlines, fly a twice-weekly service to Heathrow. N274WA is owned by World Airways of the USA and wet-leased to MAS.

Opposite below: With the landmark of Southall's gasometer visible behind the cockpit, Cathay Pacific Cargo's Boeing 747-267F SCD, B-HVZ, is ready to line-up on runway 27R for take-off.

After a very long flight from Seoul, Korean Air Boeing 747-4B5 HL-7482 is on finals for runway 09L at Heathrow.

The very pleasing design of Thai Airways'
livery is illustrated in this picture of their
Boeing 747-4D7, HS-TGR, on its way from
Terminal 3 to the take-off position for its
daily departure to Bangkok.

Flight QF2 is the Qantas midday service to Bangkok and Sydney, which on this occasion was being flown by the specially painted *Wanula Dreaming*, a Boeing 747-438. Registered VH-OJB, the aircraft is next in line for take-off on runway 09R at the beginning of its 10 –11 hour flight.

Wanula Dreaming.

On final approach from the west is this
Qantas Boeing 747-438, VH-OJJ, next to
land at Heathrow.

Air New Zealand's Flight NZ1 from Heathrow to Auckland is probably the longest of any airline using the airport. Including a stop in Los Angeles, it covers a distance of over 12,000 miles. The Boeing 747-419, ZK-NBS, will depart mid-afternoon.

Opposite above: Japan Air Lines' (JAL) daily service from Tokyo Narita, Flight JL401, is flown on this occasion by Boeing 747-446 JA8085, and is about 200 feet from touchdown at its destination.

Opposite below: Japan Air Lines' 'Super Logistics' cargo operation is a thriving part of the company's business and their Boeing 747-246F SCD JA 8132 is a regular visitor to Heathrow. In low winter light the aircraft is taxiing to runway 27R for take-off.

Opposite above: Just after midday is the departure time for the Croatia Airlines Boeing 737-230, 9A-CTC, to commence its return journey to Zagreb with Flight OU491. The aircraft is seen in Terminal 2 awaiting instructions from the tower.

Opposite below: The Hungarian airline Malev fly a twice-daily service to Heathrow. Flight MA611 is the 12.45 departure to Budapest, flown on this occasion by Boeing 737-3Y0 HA-LED, which is seen taxiing away from Terminal 2 to its take-off position.

Aeroflot Russian International Airlines increasingly use modern western-built aircraft on their long-haul services. Boeing 737-4MO VP-BAI was a welcome sight on the midday service from Moscow.

Framed between the ground signs for runway 27L, Aeroflot's Ilyushin 96, RA-96011, is lined-up perfectly for landing with Flight SU241 from Moscow.

Opposite above and below: Now the pride of Aeroflot Russian International Airlines' fleet, this 'Triple Seven', VP-BAS, is one of two which visit the airport several times per week on flights from Moscow.

Aeroflot Russian International Airlines use
both Russian and American-built aircraft on
their route between Heathrow and Moscow.
Ilyushin 86 RA-86096 is ready for her
return trip on runway 09R.

Opposite above: The attractive colour
scheme borne on this Uzbekistan Boeing
767-33PER, VP-BUZ, stands out well against
a clear blue sky. Flight HY235 originates
from the historic city of Tashkent.

Opposite below: RO392 is the Flight
number of Tarom's daily service to the
Romanian capital, Bucharest. Boeing 737-
38J, YR-BGE, is just lifting off the tarmac on
runway 09R at the start of its flight.

Bearing the French registration F-GHGE, this Balkan Boeing 767-27EER is one of two leased from Air France to give the airline increased capacity. It is operating Flight LZ495, a six-times-per-week service from the Bulgarian city of Sofia, and is about to land at Heathrow.

Very striking in its red and white livery, Lithuanian Airlines' Boeing 737-2T2, LY-BSG, makes its final approach to land on runway 27R operating Flight TE452 from Vilnius, the country's capital.

The Polish airline Polskie Linie Lotnicze, or LOT as it is more commonly known, fly several services per day from Warsaw using Boeing 737 aircraft. SP-LLD, a 400 series, is seen operating Flight LO279, on finals to runway 27L.

A CSA aircraft sits at its gate at Terminal 2 between flights. OK-WGF is a Boeing 737-4Y0.

In good winter light this Finnair Boeing
757-2Q8, OH-LBR, is next to land on
runway 09L after its flight from the Finnish
capital, Helsinki.

Another major user of the airport is the Scandinavian airline SAS. DC-9-81 OY-KHM has been pushed back from the gate at Terminal 2 in readiness for the SK508 service to Copenhagen. The airport control tower is visible in the background.

Cyprus Airways Airbus A310-203, 5B-DAR, is about to land at Heathrow on the 09.00 flight, CY504, from Larnaca.

Opposite above: On a cold January day Turkish Airlines Boeing 737-4Q8, TC-JEN, taxies towards its take-off position from runway 27R to perform Flight TK1980 to Istanbul.

Opposite below: Istanbul Airlines Boeing 737-43Q, TC-IAF, is being pushed back from gate Fox 2 in preparation for its flight to Istanbul. In service with the airline for a month, this aircraft was formerly with China Airlines.

Gathering speed down runway 09R is this
Olympic Airways Airbus A300B4-605R,
SX-BEL, with OA260, a daily return flight to
the Greek capital, Athens.

With the airport control tower in the background, Airbus A300B4-605R SX-BEK of Olympic Airways taxies from Terminal 2 towards its take-off position from runway 09R to perform Flight OA260 to Athens.

Opposite above: Taxying away from Terminal 2 is Alitalia Team's Airbus A321-112, I-BIXM, operating Flight AZ205, the 12.05 departure to Rome.

Opposite below: Alitalia's services to Rome from Heathrow are flown by Airbus A321s and McDonnell-Douglas MD-80s. I-BIXG, an A 321, is pushed from Gate F4, Terminal 2, to operate Flight AZ205 to Rome.

Substituting for an MD-80 on Flight OS453 from Vienna was this Austrian Airlines Fokker 70, OE-LFQ.

One of the busiest European routes out of Heathrow is to Frankfurt, where Lufthansa's Airbus A310-304 D-AIDH will be flying when it has been loaded.

Opposite: Lufthansa fly many services per day to Heathrow from the principal German cities using a variety of aircraft types. This Airbus A319-114, D-AILE, carries the name of the German town *Kelsterbach* and is waiting for the tower to give permission to proceed.

During the summer of 1998 France was host to the Football World Cup and won the tournament. To promote the event, several Airbus A320-211s were painted with the figure of a footballer on the fuselage. F-GJVA is an example.

Opposite above: Set against a clear blue sky, Swissair's Airbus A321-111, HB-IOF is ready to land on runway 27R after its flight from Zürich.

Opposite below: The second largest Swiss airline using Heathrow is Crossair, who were using this McDonnell-Douglas DC-9-82 on their LX825 service to Basle/Mulhouse when the author visited the airfield.

In the evening sunshine Air France's Airbus A320-211, F-GFKP, is next in line for take-off from runway 09R on a flight to Paris Charles de Gaulle.

Opposite above: Making its final approach to runway 27R, this Air Liberté McDonnell-Douglas DC-9-83, F-GJHQ, will be landing after a flight from Lyon.

Opposite below: Owned and operated by Jersey European Airlines, this British Aerospace 146-200, G-JEAS, is flown on behalf of Air France in their colours on the daily AF8833 service to Lyon Satolas.

KLM's Fokker 70, PH-KZF, has just lifted off runway 09L with the daily midday flight to Rotterdam under the code KL1334.

Opposite: KLM flights from Amsterdam are flown by Boeing 737/767s. Boeing 767-306ER PH-BZH, operating Flight KL1017, has landed on runway 09L and taxied to Terminal 4.

In low winter light, Air Portugal's Airbus A340-312, CS-TOD, taxies from Terminal 2 to the threshold of runway 27R, flying TP5153, the 12.20 departure to Lisbon.

During the summer of 1998, Air Portugal used this Airbus A320-232, CS-MAH, of their subsidiary company Air Macau on services from Lisbon to Heathrow. It proved an interesting visitor.

Opposite above and below: Cargo Air Lines, a subsidiary of El Al, were using this Boeing 747-245F, 4X-AXK, in an overall white scheme with Hertz Car Rental titles when this picture was taken. Having recently arrived at Heathrow, it is unloading its cargo.

SAS is one of six airlines who have formed a code-sharing partnership under the name 'Star Alliance'. Each company has painted one aircraft in their fleet to show the six partners. SAS Boeing 767-383ER, OY-KDH, is shown on finals to Heathrow on a flight from Copenhagen.

On a beautiful September morning Icelandair's Boeing 757-208, TF-FIN, is ready for landing on runway 27R, operating Flight FI450, the daily service from Reykjavik.